Fact Finders ™

~ The American Colonies ~

The North Carolina Colony

by Susan E. Haberle

Consultant:
Ansley Wegner, Research Historian
North Carolina Office of Archives and History
Raleigh, North Carolina

Capstone
press

Mankato, Minnesota

Fact Finders is published by Capstone Press,
151 Good Counsel Drive, P.O. Box 669, Mankato, Minnesota 56002.
www.capstonepress.com

Library of Congress Cataloging-in-Publication Data
Haberle, Susan E.
    The North Carolina colony / by Susan E. Haberle.
    p. cm.—(Fact Finders. The American colonies)
    Includes bibliographical references and index.
    ISBN 0-7368-2680-7 (hardcover)
    1. North Carolina—History—Colonial period, ca. 1600–1775—Juvenile literature. I.
Title. II. Series: American colonies (Capstone Press)
F257.H33 2006
975.6'02—dc22   2004029504

Summary: An introduction to the history, government, economy, resources, and people of
    the North Carolina Colony. Includes maps and charts.

Editorial Credits
Katy Kudela, editor; Jennifer Bergstrom, set designer, illustrator, and book designer;
    Bobbi J. Dey, book designer; Wanda Winch, photo researcher/photo editor

Photo Credits
Cover image: Farmer plowing field near Moravian settlement of Salem, North Carolina,
    The Granger Collection, New York

Collection of the Wachovia Historical Society, Photograph courtesy of Old Salem Inc., 23
Corbis/The Mariners' Museum, 4–5
Courtesy of Army Art Collection, U.S. Army Center of Military History, 26–27, 29 (right)
Courtesy of the North Carolina State Archives, 19
Getty Images Inc./Hulton Archive, 9, 29 (left)
The Granger Collection, New York, 8, 12–13, 15, 21
National Parks Service/Colonial National Historical Park, 16–17
North Wind Picture Archives, 14, 22
Rick Reeves, 10

1 2 3 4 5 6 10 09 08 07 06 05

Table of Contents

～ Chapter 1 ～

North Carolina's First People

Thousands of years ago, American Indians settled the land that is now North Carolina. By the time Europeans came, the Cherokee were the largest tribe. They lived in the Appalachian Mountains. The Catawba farmed in the central areas. The Tuscarora lived along the rivers and near the Atlantic Ocean.

Most of the American Indians ate fish. The Cherokee trapped fish in streams. Other Indians netted and speared fish in the rivers and ocean.

North Carolina Indians built their homes with materials from nature. Some built their houses with branches held together with clay. Others built log cabins.

Fish were an important food for American Indians living in North Carolina.

During the late 1600s, English settlers began to arrive and settle in North Carolina. At first, the settlers and American Indians lived together peacefully. Later, they battled each other for land.

Chapter 2

Early Settlers

In April 1585, a group of English settlers sailed to North Carolina. They landed on Roanoke Island. There, they built the first English colony in North America. This colony did not last. Within a year, the men ran out of supplies and returned to England.

The Lost Colony

John White, a settler from the first colony, traveled back to Roanoke Island in 1587. He led a group of men, women, and children to the island. The group arrived too late in the year to plant crops. White sailed back to England for supplies. The others stayed on the island.

Colonists first settled along the coast. As the colony grew, they moved inland. By 1763, North Carolina reached to the mountains. ➡

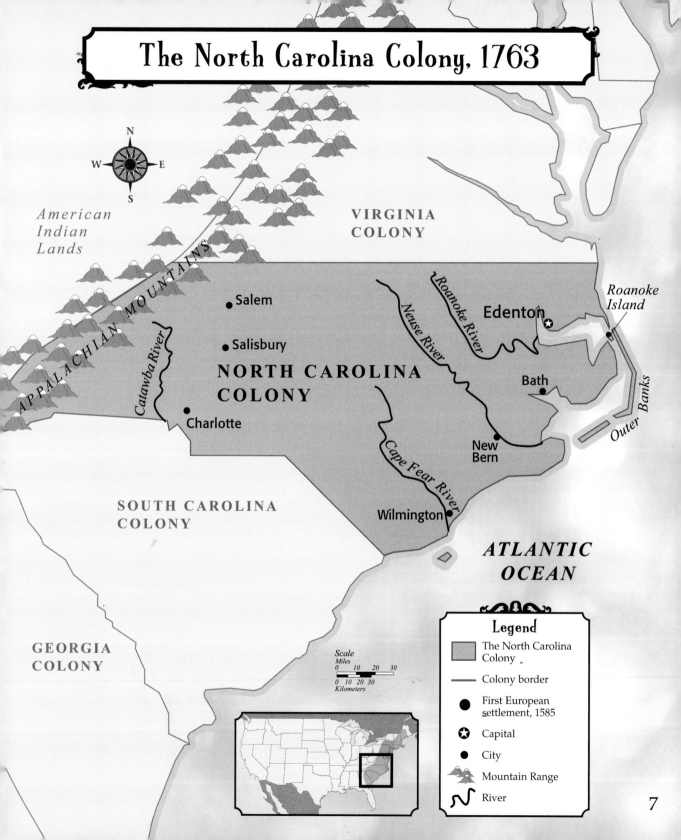

The North Carolina Colony, 1763

American
Indian
Lands

VIRGINIA
COLONY

Roanoke Island

APPALACHIAN MOUNTAINS

• Salem

Catawba River

• Salisbury

NORTH CAROLINA COLONY

Neuse River

Roanoke River

Edenton ✪

Bath •

New Bern •

• Charlotte

Cape Fear River

SOUTH CAROLINA
COLONY

Wilmington •

Outer Banks

ATLANTIC OCEAN

GEORGIA
COLONY

Scale
Miles
0   10   20   30
0 10 20 30
Kilometers

Legend

The North Carolina Colony

Colony border

● First European settlement, 1585

✪ Capital

● City

Mountain Range

River

7

Three years later, White sailed back to Roanoke. When he arrived, everyone was gone. This settlement became known as the Lost Colony.

New Colony

In 1629, King Charles I of England claimed the land that is now North and South Carolina. He named the area Carolana.

White returned to Roanoke with others and found only the word Croatoan carved on a tree. All of the colonists had disappeared. ▼

8

Around 1653, settlers moved south from Virginia to find better farmland. They were the first settlers to stay on land in what is now North Carolina.

In 1663, King Charles II of England gave a **charter** for the settlement of land he named Carolina. The king granted the land to eight Englishmen called the Lords Proprietors.

The Lords Proprietors decided not to rule the colony from overseas. Instead, they chose governors to rule the land. The colony included land in the present-day states of North Carolina, South Carolina, Georgia, and Florida.

▲ King Charles II granted the land called Carolina to the Lords Proprietors.

FACT!

The colony of Carolana was named by King Charles I of England. The king's son, Charles II, later renamed the colony Carolina.

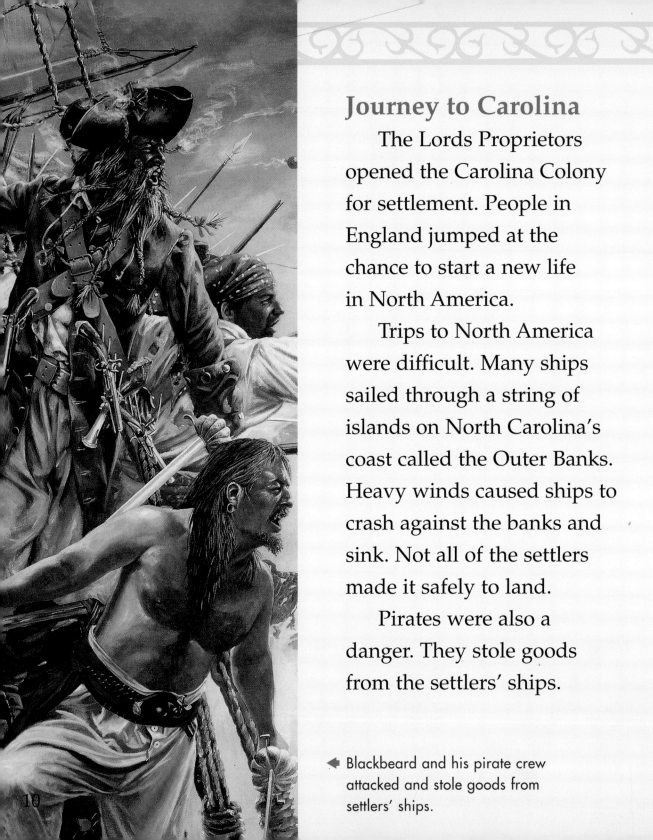

Journey to Carolina

The Lords Proprietors opened the Carolina Colony for settlement. People in England jumped at the chance to start a new life in North America.

Trips to North America were difficult. Many ships sailed through a string of islands on North Carolina's coast called the Outer Banks. Heavy winds caused ships to crash against the banks and sink. Not all of the settlers made it safely to land.

Pirates were also a danger. They stole goods from the settlers' ships.

◀ Blackbeard and his pirate crew attacked and stole goods from settlers' ships.

Many early settlers lived on farms along the coast. Land there was good for farming. In 1705, settlers started the colony's first town of Bath.

In 1712, the Lords Proprietors split Carolina into the North Carolina and South Carolina colonies. North Carolina became a British royal colony in 1729. Royal governors chosen by the king of England now ruled the colony.

Population Growth of the North Carolina Colony

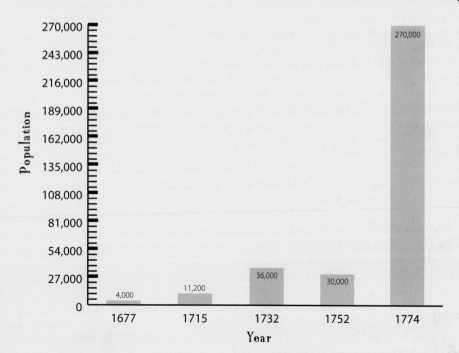

Chapter 3

Colonial Life

North Carolina colonists built their houses with wood and brick. In the early 1700s, many houses had only one room. By the mid-1700s, people were building larger homes.

Everyone in a household worked hard each day. Men worked in the fields. Women cleaned and cooked. Children planted gardens, sewed clothes, and chopped wood.

A Crop with Many Uses

The colonists were successful in growing corn. Because corn grew well, it was one of their main foods.

Many North Carolina colonists settled along the Atlantic coast.

Colonists used corn in several dishes. They boiled ground corn with water and molasses to make cornmeal mush. Sometimes they used ground corn to make a porridge called grits.

Colonists often used corn plants to make supplies. They used cornhusks to stuff mattresses. They made jug stoppers and tool handles from corncobs. People even used the cob to make corncob pipes.

The daily lives of the colonists were busy with chores. ▼

14

Schools

Like other southern colonies, North Carolina did not have a public school system. Instead, churches opened schools.

North Carolina's churches opened simple, one-room schoolhouses. Church ministers taught at these schools. Some schools were in the middle of farmland. Children worked in the fields when they were not in school.

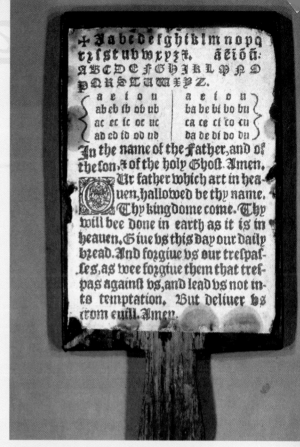

▲ In North America, children learned to read using a hornbook. Hornbooks listed the alphabet and the Lord's Prayer.

FACT!

The paper on a hornbook was covered with a clear sheet of material. This material, called horn, was made from cows' hooves.

15

~ Chapter 4 ~
Work and Trade

Most North Carolina colonists were farmers. They raised hogs and cattle. They grew sweet potatoes, beans, corn, wheat, and pumpkins to feed their families. They also raised crops that could be sold at market. Some farmers raised smaller crops of indigo and rice.

Plantations

Some colonists lived on large farms called **plantations**. Plantation owners grew cotton and tobacco. Some plantation owners bought slaves from Africa and the West Indies. They used slaves to work in their fields.

Many colonists grew their own crops to feed their families.

Farmers paid for workers to come from England. These **indentured servants** worked to pay for their travel to the colony. Servants worked for a fixed amount of time before they were free.

North Carolina Colony's Exports

Agricultural Exports

corn

tobacco

wheat

Industrial Exports

tar and turpentine

Natural Resource Exports

fish and seafood

fur

lumber

Tobacco

Tobacco was a major crop in North Carolina. Farmers shipped tobacco to England through seaports in South Carolina and Virginia. North Carolina's own harbors were too shallow for big ships.

As the colony grew, the colonists needed more land to grow tobacco. They fought battles to push American Indians deeper into the forests. The Indians were forced to move north and west.

▲ Colonists in North Carolina chopped and burned pine trees to make tar and turpentine for shipbuilding.

Other Jobs

Fishing and shipbuilding were important jobs in North Carolina. Fishers caught shrimp, crab, and herring. They shipped the fish and seafood to other colonies and England. Colonists also made turpentine and tar from the sap of pine trees. These materials were used for building ships.

~ Chapter 5 ~
Community and Faith

North Carolina did not grow as fast as the other American colonies. It had no large seaports or centers of trade. There was no easy way to get mail and goods from Europe or the other colonies.

People in North Carolina were divided by geography. Some people lived along the Atlantic coast. Other colonists lived near the mountains. Travel was difficult for settlers because so much of the colony was still **frontier**.

Wealth also divided the colony. Large landowners, small farmers, indentured servants, and slaves were all divided into separate groups.

Some colonists in North Carolina lived near the mountains. They were separated from the colonists in the lower land.

Religious Beliefs

People in North Carolina practiced many faiths. Some colonists followed the Church of England. Others were members of the Presbyterian church.

In the 1740s, many **Quakers** moved from Pennsylvania to North Carolina to farm. They settled on North Carolina's frontier where they could buy land at a low price.

◀ Quaker women often worked during church service.

FACT!

Moravians kept good records of their lives. Moravian records included many facts, such as daily weather reports.

▲ Moravians built
the town of Salem,
North Carolina.

The **Moravians** were another
large religious group that settled in
the colony. In the late 1700s, many
Moravians sailed from Germany.
They came to the American colonies
for religious freedom. In 1766, these
German colonists founded Salem,
North Carolina.

Chapter 6

Becoming a State

By the 1760s, many colonists in North Carolina were angry with the colony's British governor. People wanted more control of their local government. They were also tired of paying high taxes to Great Britain. Many families moved west into what is now Tennessee. There, they did not have to pay taxes.

In 1768, a group of North Carolina farmers from the western frontier began to speak out. They called themselves the Regulators.

In May 1771, the Regulators battled with the governor's troops. The governor needed at least 1,000 soldiers to defeat the Regulators.

North Carolina was one of the southern colonies. It was the first colony to declare its support for independence. ➡

The Thirteen Colonies, 1763

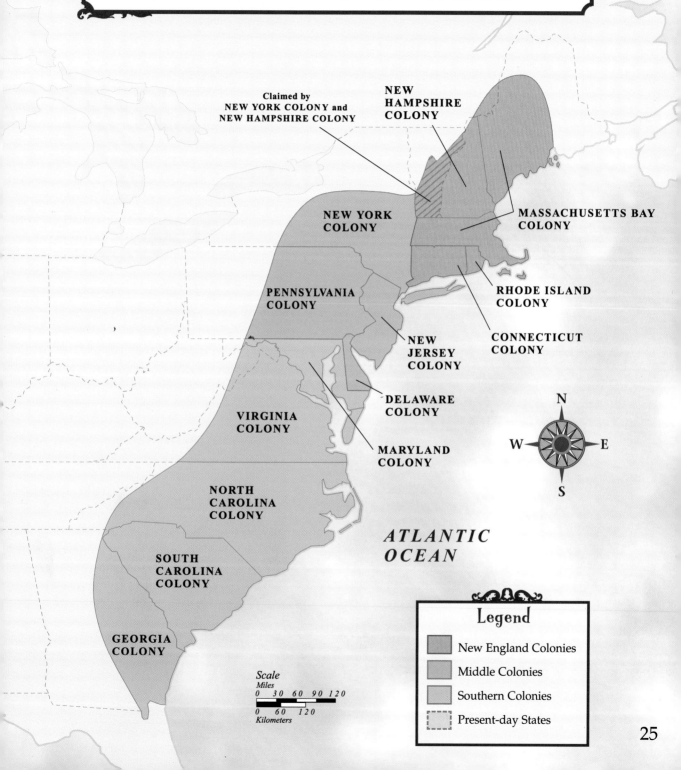

Claimed by
NEW YORK COLONY and
NEW HAMPSHIRE COLONY

NEW HAMPSHIRE COLONY

NEW YORK COLONY

MASSACHUSETTS BAY COLONY

RHODE ISLAND COLONY

CONNECTICUT COLONY

PENNSYLVANIA COLONY

NEW JERSEY COLONY

DELAWARE COLONY

VIRGINIA COLONY

MARYLAND COLONY

NORTH CAROLINA COLONY

ATLANTIC OCEAN

N
W   E
S

SOUTH CAROLINA COLONY

GEORGIA COLONY

Scale
Miles
0   30 60 90 120

0   60   120
Kilometers

Legend

New England Colonies

Middle Colonies

Southern Colonies

Present-day States

25

War with Britain

The call to end British rule spread through the American colonies. In 1774, representatives from the American colonies formed a Continental Congress. They discussed their complaints against Great Britain and what to do about them.

In 1775, war broke out between Great Britain and the colonies. Not all colonists supported the Revolutionary War (1775–1783). In North Carolina, people took different sides and battled against each other.

In 1781, North Carolina colonists fought against the British in the Battle of Guilford Courthouse. ➡

North Carolina was the first colony to announce its support of independence. On April 12, 1776, North Carolina's government adopted the Halifax Resolves. This document directed North Carolina's representatives to vote for independence.

In July 1776, the colonies announced their freedom with the Declaration of Independence. The United States won the Revolutionary War in 1783.

In 1787, Congress adopted the U.S. **Constitution** to create a stronger national government. North Carolina approved the constitution on November 21, 1789. North Carolina became the 12th state to join the United States.

Fast Facts

Name

The North Carolina Colony

Location

Southern colonies

Year of Founding

1663

First Town

Bath

Colony's Founders

Lords Proprietors

Religious Faiths

Church of England, Moravian, Presbyterian, Quaker

Agricultural Products

Corn, cotton, indigo, rice, tobacco, wheat

Major Industries

Fishing, shipbuilding

Population in 1774

270,000 people

Statehood

November 21, 1789 (12th state)

Time Line

1500s   1600s   1700s

1629
King Charles I claims
the land that is now
North Carolina
and South Carolina.

1663
King Charles II grants
Carolina to the
Lords Proprietors.

1587
John White brings
colonists to Roanoke
Island; three years later,
White returns to find
the colony deserted.

1585
Englishmen sail to Roanoke
Island; the colony lasts a year.

1707
An Act of Union
unites England,
Wales, and
Scotland; they
become the
Kingdom of
Great Britain.

1712
North Carolina
and South Carolina
split into two
separate colonies.

1763
Proclamation of 1763
sets colonial borders
and provides land for
American Indians.

1705
Colonists settle the
town of Bath.

1789
On November 21, North
Carolina is the 12th state
to join the United States.

1776
North Carolina announces the
Halifax Resolves on April 12;
Declaration of Independence
is approved in July.

1775-1783
American colonies fight for
their independence from
Great Britain in the
Revolutionary War.

29

Glossary

charter (CHAR-tur)—an official document that creates a city or colony and provides for a government

constitution (kon-stuh-TOO-shuhn)—the written system of laws in a state or country that state the rights of the people and the powers of the government

frontier (fruhn-TIHR)—an undeveloped area where few people live

indentured servant (in-DEN-churd SUR-vuhnt)—someone who agrees to work for another person for a certain length of time in exchange for travel expenses, food, and housing

Moravian (maw-RAY-vee-uhn)—a member of a Christian religious group that began in the 1400s in Germany

plantation (plan-TAY-shuhn)—a large farm where crops such as tobacco and cotton are grown

Quaker (KWAY-kur)—a member of the Religious Society of Friends, a group founded in the 1600s that prefers simple religious services and opposes war

Internet Sites

FactHound offers a safe, fun way to find Internet sites related to this book. All of the sites on FactHound have been researched by our staff.

Here's how:

1. Visit *www.facthound.com*
2. Type in this special code **0736826807** for age-appropriate sites. Or enter a search word related to this book for a more general search.
3. Click on the **Fetch It** button.

FactHound will fetch the best sites for you!

Read More

Alter, Judy. *The North Carolina Colony.* Our Thirteen Colonies. Chanhassen, Minn.: Child's World, 2004.

Coleman, Brooke. *Roanoke: The Lost Colony.* The Library of the Thirteen Colonies and the Lost Colony. New York: PowerKids Press, 2000.

Weintraub, Aileen. *Blackbeard: Eighteenth-Century Pirate of the Spanish Main and Carolina Coast.* Library of Pirates. New York: PowerKids Press, 2002.

Index